SWA.

an anthology of poetry

by

Beehive Poets

WHP

WELLHOUSE PUBLICATIONS

SWARM

Editors
Christine Bousfield and Amanda Oates.

First Edition

ISBN: 0-9547822-5-9

Published in 2008 by:

Wellhouse Publications
93 Wellhouse Lane
Mirfield
West Yorkshire
WF14 ONS

Layout----**Frank Brindle**
Cover Printing-----**Fuzz Digital,** Bradford
Binding-------**Broadbent and Tillyard,** Bradford

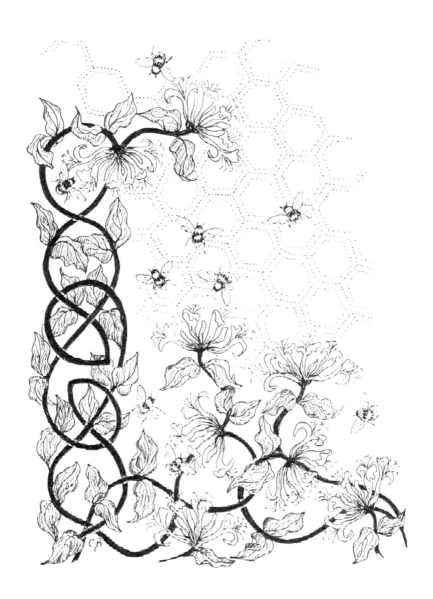

Foreword

How can we describe in a few words the multitude of voices in our fourth Beehive anthology ? There seems to be no overarching theme, though that's probably as it should be: most of us tend to avoid workshops with a definite title such as 'Leeds' or 'Death' !

In the following pages then (as suggested perhaps by our title *Swarm* and by those notorious Beehive evenings under the hissing gas lamps) you will find various murmurings, ruminations, reflections, tales with an ironic twist and, of course, enigmas (what would poetry be without them ?). They do say there's an acute shortage of bees in the world. But words, mellifluous or waspish, will never be in short supply at The New Beehive.

Our thanks to artist Jane Fielder, who very kindly allowed us to use her delightful painting of Sunbridge Road, Bradford (just down the hill from the pub) on the cover of the anthology. Thanks to Cathy Benson for the frontispiece illustration. And thanks, as ever, to Frank Brindle for his care and hard work in putting it all together, to Dr Gupta, our generous patron, to John Sugden, our devoted chairman, to our heroic landlord William Wagstaff, to Joan Burton, our proof reader, to guest poets and to the Beehive poets themselves for contributing their work.

Chris Bousfield and Mandy Oates --- Editors

Contributing Poets

Gambler

I'm a Gambling Man,
ironing my shirt, putting on
my jacket and identity,
signing in for entry

to a suite of chandeliers, cigars
and canapés, a buzz,
riffling cards, the ball rattling
in the roulette-wheel.

Youv'e seen compulsives
on a loosing run, past
the point of no return,
cashing in their last reserves.

I train my brain for shuffle-
tracking, ace tracking,
ways to beat the dealer
by memory, arithmetic.

Eyes in the sky are sharp.
A posse of security. Tap
on the shoulder. Manager:
Please leave at once, Sir.

Poker-faced, I'm back
in the high-stakes blackjack pit
with cap, moustache and walking-stick,
making only cautious bets.

My signals are discreet — a sniff,
a touch, the way I place my chips —
to let the Big Guy know when the deck
gets hot, when to make a killing.

Ed Reiss

A Small Boy

It was market day grey
and busy with the misery
of money and monotony
merchants small and tall
setting out stalls - vials
of cure-alls and punnets of vegetables

A small boy was seen amongst
the crowd something loud and
round about his appearance
though he uttered no sound
and was slight of frame, he
filled the space of a well
fed man and walked with a
gait of unfathomable confidence

The boy said nothing
no voice, no cry of pain
no joyless exclamation
he led by the example of his smile

Passing paupers piss soaked
lepers whose faces were
ravaged by life
the barrow boys, the minstrels
even the jesters wore turned up gashes and
painted on laugh lines

He walked by baulking
veterans of ordinary wars

yawning jaws of boredom
and indifference

Past dusty halls of
ceremony and sterile
sanctimony
a priest turned up his
old pope nose
as he went amongst
the spent stench of
endless benches
the tents of his
rarefied robes
the cold stones of walls and floorings

The priest chewed the cud
of disgust
never had he seen such
blasphemous happiness

Trimmed and prim, trussed
and tucked, the ladies
in the front row groaned
on their bare pews
of hardened yew trunks

No words did the boy utter
no butter to appease his masters
no cross hot execrations
or cynical condemnations
he did not seek to

praise or flatter nor
did he wish to hurt
or hamper no cant
or rant or pomp or
chant of holy lamentation

He did not stamp his
feet or slam his fist hard
upon the pulpit
he did not scorn or
scowl, gurn or howl
his face stayed fixed
and passive

And when they had all
turned to look at him (one by one)
up and down passing their judgements
the boy spun on the
ball of his heel and
left the way he came
with a smile on his face

Michael Stewart

The deep

Kirkstall Bridge Design Centre

Inside the bottle on the windowsill
under the surface of its standing water
cars and buses swim by upside down
in a parabola within its fisheye lens.

Up to the front in turn they lunge,
swell up, then shrink back down and off:
red mail van, orange access bus,
unmarked white transit, topped with ladders.

Between and beyond, along the pavement
from right to left a woman in a plum coat
passes the rugby pitch where, almost
too small to make out, four seagulls

and a crow practise manoeuvres
as a lad in pale blue jeans sits on the wall
by the bus stop drumming his trainers,
unaware of his underwater life.

Julia Deakin

Blue

Mother

of all things blue

undress my eyes and then

let me sink or swim at your breast

the waves

F. Brindle

Fowl Language

When a toe is stubbed
the head jerks and the elbows jut,

and with it, close to a cluck,
Fuck. Fuck. - Fuck. Fuck.

Andrew Fentham

Lugworms

I watched the force of his workman's boot
stamp his spade into the sand, the lean back
on the handle then up with the load. A twist
and the heap of dark sand, black on top,
was piled by his left foot.
He searched with his finger and thumb, found one,
grunted and shook the sand off it.
Its muscular body slowly writhed in the air.
He dropped it onto a seething pile, a bait-pail
full of twists of rubber, each trying to get
under the cover of its neighbour.

I copied him, stamped my sandal down hard
on my spade, more used to its sandcastling,
leant it back, heaved up the load
twisted it onto the beach, but couldn't touch.
With a razor shell and my spade I lifted
the worm into my bucket. It looped about
like a knot untying, red-bristled middle,
black at both ends, more solid than an earthworm
the way weeds are tougher by the shore.

All afternoon we dug for more, working to beat the tide.
The beach was full of coils of sand. He pointed out
the nearby holes, holes to breathe. "Dig between them".
Every coil had one, inches away, like a full stop.
I saw some open and close, just a spurt of grains.
He drew a U-shape with his finger, their burrow.
"They eat sand, fish eat them, you eat fish," he said.
But I knew fish were milky flakes in my mouth.
Tried not to think of hooks.

Cathy Benson

Lament for Jimmy Knut

A helluva tuff guy
from Minnesota, he knows
what's what, but don't talk:
he won't talk, whatever,
whatever they do, and what they do,
it's unspeakable.

           It's indescribable
what's going on, what's behind the door,
the closed door, the heavy, black door,
the door with a round, brass knob, a knob
that turns.

A hand turns
the round brass knob, pushes,
pushes open the heavy, black door.
It's a hand in a kid glove.

           It waves aside
the apelike men, waves them aside,
the brass-knuckled apelike men, the men
who like nothing, who like nothing
like beating a guy to pulp.

           The hand,
the hand in a kid glove, pulls on the head,
pulls on the head of a helluva tuff guy,
pulls gentle, looks into the face, the pulped face,
this face from Minnesota.

"He's a helluva tuff guy, this guy. This
guy from Minnesota, a helluva tuff guy.
He's one tuff cookie.
                          And he knows
what's what," says the Boss,
says the Big Boss, hand tight
in a kid glove. It's a hand pulling
on the head of a dead guy.

He's a dead guy:
                     he shoulda stayed
where he was, stayed in Minnesota,
stayed planting alfalfa,
                          picking maize,
cucumbers and toe-mate-toes,
stayed in Minnesota picking toe-mate-toes,
picking big, red, juicy toe-mate-toes.

Ain't nowhere like Minnesota, nowhere
in the world like Minnesota for toe-mate-toes,
nowhere, not for big, red, juicy
toe-mate-toes.

Steve King

By Drowning

He weaves his way
around it.
Writes endless lists
but never pins it down
never picks it up
never lets it hang
trembling from a fist
and says
this is
what's happening.
This has got to stop.

He could be merciless
drown it
like a kitten
take a nifty
little pistol
shoot it
in the head
but he chooses
the slow
humane approach:
with lavender
hypnosis
seals his mouth
with Gaffa tape
weaves his fingers
into cold racks
of traction
or spreads it out
as carrion for dogs.

It's in him now.
He bleeds
he pisses, he weeps.
It won't wash out.
It clouds his blood
clogs his cells
taints his lips
each letter of it
etched into his rib cage
will infiltrate his heart
until he's dead.

Gaia Holmes

The Transformation

She opens her mouth
and all the angels
come out singing
and he feels like
something
that's been dropped
in front of her,
a crumpled mistake,
like something
that has crawled
through the moors
with sacks of gloom
on his back,
scratches on his face,
wizened gnats
and husks of ling
tangled in his hair
and he is dumb
knowing that his notes
are all bent and crippled,
burnt and off key.
Love
would thud
blackly from his lips
like a threat,
like something
from the back of a crow.

So
the softening process
begins.
He tames
his starched heels
with honey,
sleeps with nightingales
in his throat,
stained glass
beneath his tongue,
meditates
on the glister
of a pomegranate heart
and learns to buffer
the angles of his life
with silence.

Gaia Holmes

Sheep

Twat one at 50
and it bursts like a blood-rug,
splits like dropped shopping,
swills its soup over camber, skid-flung stones.

You crack cud, buckle the cobbles of its bleat,
A stammer-slab of mard green sound
shatters, scatter-guns the tax disc like a gritter's truck
as it bunk beds, pikes, stunned stiff,
cabers, wigbags tongue-flung.

Fleas lose their jungle disco.
Their bitten dance floor stiffens.
They feel an oven die.

Now it could be anything:
A dead cloud, billow of a bin bag
the last, cold stubborn shout of snow.

Nothing moves - just wool, one wisp, still warm
burrs the Volvo's bumper
tattoos a surrender over skid mark, zinging chrome,
the confetti of still stunned stones.

Michael Greavy

Better

I can tell talk from better;
blindfolded, I know that
'fair to middling' is where
the dodgems skitter,
no-one really wanting to
crash head on. 'Not so bad',
in its plain brown wrapper,
hides colours that you must feel
I don't trust 'mustn't grumble',
that sweet when the larder's empty.
Better tastes like no one else,
like the yellow of sunshine on
your pillow, or in a buttercup field,
a cow nuzzles your hand,
saying 'this is what you're made of'.

Bruce Barnes

Autumn Trout

Water -
black as a graveyard cough
and maggot disco, itch the sling
whiplash in my letting go
skitter, scud the iron air
spark the dying edge of things
and windbend, bomb like rubber snow
down through autumn's copper laugh
the fizz and jig of midge.

Red reflections blink them in
as mud-bound, unloved, drowned
they hula, scribble, wag and chug
doodle through the trout-thought lounge.

Gone, I still imagine them:
fat rice flung at weddings
scatter-sunk, slung under bronze
done in down the pond's bad end
by the brutal, sudden gift of fins.

Michael Greavy

Because,

'cos' might be a gardener's tired wake-up call,
a wet lettuce slapped across the lethargic screen,
saying the climate is changing and what are we,
innocuous viewers, at the grubby end
of finger pointing doing; no doubt, muting the sound,
making our excuses, and leaving fault fiddling
with the channel changer, hurdling responsibility
dozing on the couch, as we pop out for some air.

Outside is huge,
huger still because we are set down in it,
to read the snail's script on the red tiles gleam;
but we are not of it, the night sky elbows us
on the doorstep. We linger with so many stars,
like coach lagged tourists: if this is the world,
it must be Thursday. The wheelie bins agree,
dark outlines leaning into the wind, steadied
by our rubbish, and looking like priests. But they can't forgive us

the sin of emission.
No, we've not forgotten the 'O' that's in wonder,
that is keeping us a doorstep removed from stars,
that lets the snail slide one step ahead of understanding,
but, in our lonely frailty, we have gathered
anything that can survive us, enough that is
indestructible, too much for tonight's bear hug
to embrace. Only *because* wholly degrades,
degrades to empty excuses.

Bruce Barnes

Blackbird

Some times are best left to their own devices;
sometimes, they will gather up what seemed the small hours,
and squeeze them into a packed moment to catch
your breath. In that time, all the time is a blackbird
singing for dear life, and you didn't think he could
be responsible, but there's your counterpoint begging,
'Sing on'. Stopping then would be.... almost unthinkable...
breathing into the unreserved quiet of sometime,
the feel of new, and you would have to begin again.

Bruce Barnes

Upon the Death of Anthony Ashley-Cooper, 10th Earl of Shaftsbury

Along with Kremlin poisonings in London
good still to see earls on the Rochester route,
roaring and rolling down the French Riviera.

Reading of his death on a train I, drear
and nomad, feel the anvil kiss of identity
and the sense diffused that rises in the chest
like a brazen weltschmerz and touches everything.

Out of the city, away from the BT tower and
the Bullring's bends and warps; out toward steeples,
round the backs of houses, dilapidated sheds and allotments;
further to early rapeseed, ridiculous and toxic;
I am splayed by my faux-Sartrean mull.
In places neither Midland nor Northern are
grassy clumps in marshpools like drowned buffalo,

caravan parks by knowing medieval waters,
crawling and calling and brown. We pass fields
that one day, for the first time, will not exist.

Before long it's Yorkshire's cusp: bandied
wooden aitches, pale stone and a slight dip down.
I step off at Leeds and a man lights a cig from England's Glory.
There's a scuffle with a porter and I walk into the city.

Andrew Fentham

Where the soul of man . . . .

Well, it ain't Memphis.
So, maybe we're up river a-ways,
a warm night, St Paul, Minnesota,

when Maybellene,
late shift checkout queen,
scans the yoghurt and fruit, yet
stops short of a cutting remark -

there's just something
about this old-timer, sorting
for change in the torn pocket
of a faded gold lamé jacket
hanging loose about his midriff

as he runs a hand
through thinning hair,
dyed black and swept back,
forelock hanging loose,
apologizing: he's short two bits.

Well, hell! she don't know why,
but she tells him forget it,

and he says: "Thank you, ma'am,
that's mighty fine of you."
before walking away, slow,
rhythmical from the hips,
that po' boy slink,

                    and his smile
- it makes her want to forget
those too many miles on her clock.

He's like a fine, ol' Cadillac
a-phut-phut-phuttering
about the parking-lot,
exhaust billowing into the neon haze.

Steve King

Clinging On: Lunchtime in the Seaview Café

Trimmed neat to meet a thick glossed picture rail
anaglypta, distempered pink & turquoise,
colour without intensity, overwhelming the eye
as it drains the soul.

It's a workmanlike job in a world where solidity counts,
where craft & cleanliness fill in for affluence
- no-nonsense chairs, tables, tightly jointed
& simple wall-lights. Everything perfectly well designed,
but for the occasional flourish, a floral motif
squandered here, there, an attempt to banish austerity.

& you do get value for money – cold ham (if sliced thin,)
chips, tea, bread & butter, condiments provided, half a crown, all
in:

"Sorry, no peas, no carrots. It's a café dear, not a restaurant."

It's where a man can smoke down to the stub
without once taking the roll-up from between his lips
or his hands from his pockets.

Where the cardigan stays buttoned beneath his suit jacket,

& where his wife, her NHS wig, tight-curled, monstrously coal-
black,
examines her cuticles,
tries to remember when it was, the last time they ate out,
before breaking the silence between them.

Steve King

Birthday

Not the one when our eyes first see
The light of our very first day. No.
The one where the table is set for celebration,
candlelight reflected in a mirror, a haloed flame.
A birthday, a prism splitting years into joys and sorrows.
Unfocus. See glimmers of tomorrows where highs
and lows lie like ammonites curled
in future memories, waiting.

This moment is every moment: the fulcrum of the seesaw,
the cog in the roundabout, the height of the swing.
It's the fallback of a wave with its memory
of the beach and gathering up into the next swell.
It's the eye of a needle waiting a thread;
a stitch in a tapestry showing us our history.
This moment is in the candle flame
before we blow it out. Wish well.

Cathy Benson

Palm Houses

My parents visit Kew. They pay their penny,
sit at the crossing of Africa and the Americas;
banana trees, the fruits my father unloads.
'Musa acuminata' he mouths. 'Canary bananas.'
'Musa xparadisiaca, enand gigante. Plantain.'

She, due to bear eight children, fingers dioscarea;
'a major contribution to the development of contraception.'
But this plant will be only for her daughters and grandaughters.
She licks the sounds of custard apples; 'ananna cherimola,'

Children are calling in The Palm House.
Cotton will unfold; 'Gossyium herbaceum, var.africanum ,'

Back in Sefton Park, my parents linger
near the Monsterosa Baja. Panes of glass reflect
them young and hopeful. They hold hands on a bench,
in sweaty humid air. Recite the names of ships;

Lusitania, Mauritania, Princess Royal.
Their hands are dry, hers from bannisters
in big houses, his from flour sacks, asbestos.

He'll tell her of bananas as big as your arm,
spiders, parakeets, 'and you should see the size of the rats.'
He offers a cigarette. Gets out a ring. She contemplates
years of such polishing, stairs. Inhales.

Kath Mckay

Pomegranates

These are late summer fruits.
The shopkeeper sets a handful
in an arc to divide fruit from fruit
buffer the thick clay of roots
from the porcelains of white and purple
aubergines, plums holding tight
their blood blister juices.

Fat bellied candle-holders
they sit above wasp-waisted pears
their rinds yellow with housemaids' calluses.

These are Persephone's fruits:
complex as a scooped out brain.
They cup darkness beneath their skins
bleeding into themselves.

Their juice is regret, remembering
her lips. The winter sun dropping
like a ripe fruit. Her foot
always on the downward stair.

Sue Wood

Lazy Villanelle (August)

I'm sitting in a deck chair, having a little think,
And idly watching two huge dragon flies,
And wondering who will bring me a nice long cool drink,

I've left the washing up in the kitchen sink
The kids are out playing; I can hear their distant cries.
I'm sitting in a deck chair having a little think.

From my neighbour's garden I can hear that icy clink;
I see his loaded tray with envious eyes,
And wonder: Might *he* offer me a nice long cool drink?

My skin is slowly turning a horrid shade of pink
But it's far too much bother to shift or rise
I'm sitting in a deck chair having a little think.

Ask me what I'm thinking. I'll tell you with a wink.
And when you hear my answer it'll come as no surprise
I'm thinking: Who will bring me a nice long cool drink?

I'm too lazy to move, can't even even be bothered to blink.
I'm waiting for a breeze and studying the skies,
Lolling in my deck chair, having a little think,
And wondering who will bring me a nice long cold cold drink.

Gerard Benson

34

Dutch

The hand of Holland man is everywhere.
Lines head straight for right angles in polderland,
town squares. Mondriaan canals grid the nation.

In Den Haag water lily lawns are cut to oblongs.
Through the leafy Hagen Bos unlikely men in suits and ties
pedal with intent in the lime dappled glow..

A grey heron models stick thin chic.
Curves come in full circles: cycle wheels, cheeses,
plates, pancakes, oranges in pictures.

These level headed flatlanders' sense of light and dis-
tance
pushes boundaries with a quiet force
where nature is giving in to man at the edge of the
garden.

Mandy Oates

SIFNOS

what stirs this is-

land? - humming through my days
as flowers in their beds
are bumbled or

borrowing that cr-
inkled ribbon-cirrus for
outcrops headless with ocean

where this head itself bobs on
hock from some three-
fingered hand held

out to africa - ah
my mountain was raised
quick as a child — this ninefold

stomach grumbles to collapse
houses & my night is
slow arousal from

sleepless light - yet in
hills loud with dark these
wings have fanned the hive &

my legs jointed & japanned in
death kept frantic survival
hollow & at bay &

i lean into all small
winds eye scale palp fun
-nelled to the roar that raised me

here to stream with seas on all
sides which etch me blue
till i cannot bear this

hourglass sac of self i
believe i am whose nape is a
sifting through of head to trunk -

thus do i disbar these sands for
keeping eyes wide falls
toward dream &

even watch-
fulness must out
-strip time - outgrow self to

sometimes dream

Mario Petrucci

Cave Paintings (for Colin Widdup)

You kept musk oxen,
their shaggy coats and small curved horns
from cave paintings lit by torchlight.
They breathed early morning mist,
rust red shapes swaying
as they tucked in their hooves
and settled heavily among the cabbages.
I remember how they looked at me
and I took a plaster of paris cast
of their absence indented
on the earth among the cabbages.

Genny Rahtz

Mellifont

He has an emphatic voice, the tour guide,
and it's raining hard, so we're sheltering
in a ruined medieval chapel, listening
to a litany of facts. But we're dry inside,
like the dates and the names of unknown men —
monks, builders, cow-men, saints — he's drumming
into our ears. Watching waterdrops dripping
from the stone lintel, I hesitate, then
make my bid and step straight past the others
into the outside, into weather and air;
stone shapes stand on the green, grey as the sky,
the eloquent calligraphy of those dead brothers,
a message, cryptic, saved for a rainy day —
broken doorway, row of arches, half a stair.

Gerard Benson

Every Time

Every time I step
from the medium of this dry breath
from land to water
I am reclothed
in the movement of liquid on my skin.
My spine elongates,
relinquishes its load
to outstretched limbs,
awakens bodily memory.

And as I swim,
my breathing amplified
excites molecules of breath
exhaled from remote human ancestors
as they fished the tides
their long hair
rising and falling on the sea,
hair dripping
as they climbed to open caves
could still hear the crunch
of predator on shingle.

They watched over the sea
and synchronised their breathing
with the waves
felt cocooned in slow pulse
tidal rhythms,
boom of sea caves.

Genny Rahtz

LITTLE DEATH LATE CLASSICAL STYLE

It's all about sex, he said, guiding
her fingers over the keys. First the Exposition -
a couple of motifs playing in counterpoint, opposition
rather than dialogue. Then Development,
an inevitable slide into the dominant,
subdominant resistance from the treble
becoming shrill, hysterical,
tension building into crisis,
unresolved arpeggios, broken chords.
She's worn down in the end - listen to those responses,
you know you want to, can't keep this up,
yes I can, no you can't, give in, give in,
you must, you will, no,... oh all right then,
rallentando, resolution, perfect cadence.

Chris Bousfield

Hermit

He's a hermit
in what is arguably
the leading hermit colony
in the country.

It's a charity
run by a lady
who hand-picks each hermit
personally.

She gives each one a cave.
She brings the food and often stays
until it's too dark
to get back.

They have a sense of balance there.
And that is good for him — and good for her.

Ed Reiss

LET AGE...

They happened while sleeping
hieroglyphs on my face;
as the shadows were deepening,
someone else took my place.

Hieroglyphs on my face:
I'm not long for this earth,
someone else took my place,
someone bom at my birth.

I'm not long for this earth,
someone else took my place,
someone bom at my birth
who looks out of my face.

Someone else took my place,
I fall out of time,
she looks out of my face
and this flesh is not mine.

Chris Bousfield

Scrupulous

In the bookshop, in the Sport section,
I notice beside me a woman:

comely, curvy body, look
that's mischievous, melancholic.

She's got a pile of books, including
The Little Book of Flirting,

Successful but Something Missing?
and *How to Make Anyone Fall in Love with You, Right Away,*

I'd make a move, say something
witty and non-threatening

if only I could think of something
witty and non-threatening to say.

Ed Reiss

Under the Pear

They wore flowered cotton dresses
ankle socks, crêpe-soled sandals and the sun was high
and on their nut-brown legs the silver down of hairs
sparkled in the light that lasered through the ancient
barn
from jagged holes, yellowing the musty ground.

They stared, and reassured him with words.
The younger, bolder one reached out
to touch the prepuce, then, with thumb and finger
pushed it back across its rigid stem
She slowly sat back on a tilted beam
and spread her legs, examining herself.

The 'let's pretend' was wrapping it in leaves
broad green assegai, gathered from the rank mounds
piled outside the barn. They held it then
to heal. They were excited and on edge
and when they left the barn to carry on
the operation; under the ovoid globes of ripening
pears
within the shadows of an ageing tree
the older one sat motionless and troubled on the swing
staring before her, with intensity.

F. Brindle

Easter Sunday

Dog.
Blood-water mongrel.
Lying stone in river,
alone.

Coaxed,
charmed.
sold by water's hoax.

Rushes,
puppy-pushed with thirst.

A drink,
a dram,
tippling,
young, mixing the swirl.

Water nips up, shimmies,
sussing,
slips him a souse.

Another douse,
dog dosed, wants out.

Pickling in the whiskey slug.

Babbles,
bobs for branch,
bites a bow-wow,
stuck on stick.

Twig-swigging.
Brook tickling in its catch.

Dog drowned on Easter Sunday.
Buried in water, alone.
An unsoiled grave
with a stick for a stone.

Francis Byrne

Scared

Coward
the ditch is not deep
Jump
there are no eyes
glinting
in the shadows
Sleep
and another thing
the stars are not
likely to hurtle down
in flaming balls
and destroy the town
Grow up.

I grew up
went to war,
made the flaming stars fall
was a glint
in the shadows
the destroyer of sleep
made a chasm
so deep it could
not be crossed
in a thousand years
and I am not scared at all.

Nuala Robinson

Canis familiaris

He is curled, mid-way between
two human bodies and the fire
a sodden toy inert beside his paw.
Eyes close, ears sag, the muscles slack beneath
articulated landscape of his fur.
And behind his eyes, he sees
the open fields
a narrow curling pathway under trees.

The present is for waiting in, as now
for feet, beyond the door
for Jane arriving with her Labrador
bringing again the now familiar routes
that lead across a world of scents
vaporous air, testosterone and pheromones
that ghost around the clumps and roots
the posts and trunks and piles of doo.

Opportunity and threat
all Orphean promise and regret
whilst tethered to the short leap back
into the car then down
the driveway to the fire
a nether world of being
neither, partly human
or completely dog.

F. Brindle

a homecoming

spring rain is as warm as tears on my face
the tarmac under my feet like treading grapes
a PA is playing the call to prayer
I pass the mosque and the massage parlour.
I stop and rest outside the abattoir
Over the road from the Craven Heifer
A builder's bricking up the back window
There's a crow picking meat off the road.
I pass a pound shop with a spring sale on:
Where everything is less than a pound.
A woman is feeding scabby pigeons
the scraps from the last of her Happy Meal,
I pass dossers in doorways - their lives furled
Only their dogs look out at the world.

Michael Stewart

Flooded Out

First sign of the pest is curious gear
littering the porch. Watch out before
it can breach your inner dam. Never
allow space to a fisherman, whether
lover or lodger.

His keepnet folded in the hall extends
six feet when a heel gets caught in it.
Weights skitter round washing machines.
Bags of feed spill to clutter doorways.
Maggots turn to flies.

Even what is yours will get pulled in,
lunch boxes punctured to aerate worms,
scissors and camping stools purloined,
socks holed, outdoor clothes patterned
with silver sequins.

Rivers, becks converge from all sides,
bidding to cascade through your rooms.
Dace, chub, roach flap on the carpets.
Whiskery barbel with dead men's faces
loom from mirrors.

Simon Currie

everyone remembers where they were

Everyone remembers where they were
the day JFK was blown away
and the day Diana died,

so they say.
I was still off-stage in 1963,
waiting to make my entry.

But the day that Diana passed away
I was levelling a patient
on a secure ward.

A piercing scream drew me to the dayroom.
Where one man was laughing,
and another man was crying.

The crying man was pointing at the television,
the laughing man was pointing at him.
I gave the crying man a coffee, and a cigarette.

Through the smoke of a comforting Regal
the face of Diana in retrospect.
The man calmed down

It was clear that the Princess
was not his favourite soap character,
She had died the week before.

Michael Stewart

Nice work

In here I'm trying to write a poem
while out there a man has come
to clean the hall and landing carpet.
Paul Armitage's Home Cleaning Service,
van in drive, is feeding two diameters of hose
in through the windows, one sucks
while the other blows apparently
and *is it OK if I run the hot tap?*

In here I'm trying to write a poem
going back in time two thousand years.
Out there he *no I'm fine love, no,
no problem* starts up the compressor
In here I'm hewing granite, out there
he squirts detergent on each stair in here
I'm hauling monoliths uphill on logs
out there he *may have to move the piano
slightly*

In here I'm chanting pagan funeral rites
out there I notice two different tones of suck
then intermittent thuds, clicks and bumps
advancing on the door which I get up and close,
properly, wondering how long
the quarrying took. Out there he's *going
to have to try the bathroom window*
in here I - oh, sod it.

Julia Deakin

RABBITS

Towards twilight they emerge
from burrows in a sandy bank
like a block of Gruyère cheese.

Dog always has a rabbit in front,
one rabbit has dog right behind,
but rabbits are diving down drifts
and others bolt out of more holes.

How many rabbits does dog chase,
does one rabbit decoy for another
and do they communicate a plan?

Why does dog never stop running,
sit down and work it out?

John Sugden

DECEMBER

December, still named the tenth month
after hundreds of years of fallen leaves.
The winter solstice, chain saws busy,
hedgehogs slumber under composts,
A stray ladybird survives on a blind.

John Sugden

On Addingham Moor

Our landscape guru, expert no doubt
on medieval sites, is no geologist.
He seems to think these boulders,
snapped from the scarp above,
are true erratics, brought by glacier.
Worse, he labels them "erotics",
not once but twice, oblivious.

We snigger, bad as kids at school,
leaning against millstones
that broke or proved too thick,
like obelisks at Luxor
or Easter Island statues.
"What's so funny then?" he asks.
Can millstone grit be frivolous?

Abrasive, black-bleak slabs
make this a harsh work-place
for masons once, surveyors now.
But thirty miles away, at Norber,
real erratics step down at night
from their limestone pedestals,
to join in cumbersome embrace.

Simon Currie

NO RELEVANT MOUTHS?

As at the centenary they discuss your place
in the canon or establishment
you wear a suitable face.
Surprise and disappointment

cross your brow like grikes,
the clints deeply etched.
Your head inclined to the right
(should it have been to the left?)

lines up with lopsided Windsor.
Your ears are of a proportion
that frightens me even to whisper.
Your nostrils quiver at our situation.

Your hair is surprisingly dark, eyes curtained,
bagged with boys and vermouth.
Your wide mouth is downturned.
Remember Spain: enough is enough.

John Sugden

Halfway

There is no rhythm to your movement
Only imagined reason.
Still it is a communication of sorts.
Described best in old language.
A quickening.

Some reciprocation for the worry
The new realms of anxiety
An altered centre of gravity.
A rediscovering of wonder,
Reprioritising the future.

Holding our hearts already,
We run ahead of you.
Picturing sports days and first steps.
Before formal introductions
We find you here already.

Sarah Wilson

Slice

Before they built this terrace in the 1870s
they kept pigs on this patch of land,
the owner big in butchery, whose shop
on Harehills Road fed servants
from the big houses Moortown way, and
non-observant Jewish garment workers.

Hard to picture, here, where the row has stood
a century and seen off several tenants' decors,
that beneath the carpeted front parlour and above
the level of the cellar set-pot, the soil
these were dug from sustained pigs, the ground worn
to the precise consistency pigs like, to feel at home.

It's built up now and traffic-bound, the only trace
of 'Woodland View' a few park trees. Evenings,
in our dark green papered living room
with its bay window seat and art nouveau
tiled fireplace, we listen, between sputters
from the frosty little gas fire, for the snuffling.

Julia Deakin

Anniversary

Today you told me it was over a year,
12 months and more of living together.
It seems less and more.

Less, because we fitted so easy
Beneath the cosy blanket of domesticity
Spooning together ying and yang.

More, it was a rough year
A year I would not wish on any soul
With the deaths and the desperation.

I cannot imagine anyone else now.

Sarah Wilson

Letter Found in a Stevie Smith Biography

Dad
if you have this book
or really don't want to read it
please please take it back
and choose something else.

We won't be insulted at all.
We just much prefer
to pick something personally
than get you a book token.

We spoke to the lady in
The Toll House Bookshop (Holmfirth)
just to be sure
you could change it.

She knew you of course
very well and said
there's no problem
and wished you a tip-top day.

Andrew Fentham

Day Patient

Maggie, who will tell you
that your shorn head is beautiful?
You who chose a sleek chestnut wig
from a rack of curls
amongst other protheses?

I remember your real hair
soft tawny mouse
thinned to wisps around your ears
lived-in, at home.
Then an absence, your easy chair
given up to another
his belly large with its terrible fist of cells.

Today you return, pale as if
you had lain in a deep sea-cavern
watching light freckle the darkness.
Your blood alight
your body a circlet of pin-point suns.

You wear the wig.
I come into the treatment room
to retrieve my pen
as you lift off that helmet
your head is as fine as a bird's skull
neck poised, warrior queen
staked to the flames.

Sue Wood

Trespassing

That day we walked on the beach with the Danger sign
we were 100K south of Sydney,
Cut down a side road: 'Achtung.
No entry.' Silence. Hundreds
of dead birds, banked like shoes,
waves sucking. Somewhere behind,
the hum of the motorway. Us
with our mouths open, the sweet smell
of death. 'Must have been recent.
Better leave before the rats come.'

And so we went on: a log cottage,
teacups laid out for us. Chocolate biscuits.
Parakeets,

Kath Mckay

BREAD

For weeks
he's been raw-eyed
and monkish,
living on plain potatoes
flakes of rust
and Holy water
pilfered
from the Parish font,
devoted - anointing
her angst
with his prayers,
wrapping
the memory of her
in softness
and alibis
but tonight
his piety's absolved.
Love cracks and twists
into something
with teeth and claws
and he wants bread.
He could eat a horse,
a house, a baby.

He wants to
gouge his nails
through the crust,
sink his fingers
into the dough
until he finds
a heart
worth hooking.
He wants to
pretend he is
a devil
with a belly
full of stone.

Gaia Holmes

Early frost

She practises the piano because we say
it will be something for her when
she is grown-up or maybe on her own.

We compose her future, or so she thinks
and practising will bring the notes and everything
to that clear point ahead. Her hands comply.

Frost outlines the garden behind
as she sits in her red dressing gown
feet just touching the pedals.

I stand behind the door and listen
'Fur Elise' comes in its slow, repeated melodies.
In her fingers there is a sadness she cannot know

yet stumbles into, her slippered feet
unwilling in the cold. Outside the window
emptied earth and a sharp October frost.

Sue Wood

The Last Weekend

I remember watching the Pope
on a balcony, doing an impression
of Sooty: and thinking, that despite
the intoning commentator
that it was not a dignified death.

We arrive at the ward as visiting closes
and loiter around: half expecting;
perhaps hoping to be turned away.
What lies beyond the curtain breeds fear.

He is happy to see me, his twisted
face and toothless grin, combine
with his newly chemo'd hair
to give him the air of a parrot.
Harsh but fair. He loves animals.

The last attack, the one which should
have killed him, has withered his legs
to skeletal reminders of Japanese cruelty;
and like the Pope, I am reminded of
glove puppets: no strings attached.

I am too emotional to deal with
my cousin and my aunt, who chatter
at us, as if this were a wedding.
I bury myself in newsprint; read twice.

I have consoled myself in many ways.
I am thankful for the peace
that allows me to bury my father:
though my counselling sessions hint
at the war in which he buried me.

And then we are alone. My mother,
and my girlfriend, go to find tea
and company, and with them goes
my daughter: secure in the belly
that keeps her from his arms.

For nearly forty years we have
swung from silence to anger and
onto indifference. Now I make
small talk. The tumour on his brain
prevents his reply.

I talk of village gossip, but
mainly I talk of my daughter.

I see by his face that he approves.
I burble and flow like a bore
encouraged by the stroke ridden smile.

That night at the club I am asked
how he is. I do not hide his death.
My mother calls it passing and
hides from the world; I understand.

The ritual of the bar; the gossip
and the laughter, the absence of weakness
and the drone of the kareoke
cannot be easy for her. As her love
slips to memory like bubbled beer.

He is again pleased at my coming.
But the stay is shorter. He needs
changing, and it pricks the soap bubble
line between illusion and his dignity.

I make hurried excuses. Forced from
my chair by a bolt of electricity,
at not wanting my memory to be of my father
as a man in a hospital bed; hovering
between infantilism and death.

I take his hand for the last time.
I stoically smile for the last time.
I look into his eyes for the last time.
My last image of him, is a man
recognisable as my father, with tears
in his eyes; his spirit rising
from the bed to follow me.

I do not speak for a long time.
Not until we drive from the hospital
grounds, navigate the round-a-bout
pass the crem and reach the turkey factory.

Jeremy Young

SIFNOS

one sailing

i am - this steady light of boat
ruddered upward through
dark by flame

as though sea
took to verticals so
one flicker might float &

as all creeps downward that
lone stub-mast draws
other sails to

steer by its light
or cast nets together &
strengthen prows on dark like

hands prayered towards water
or a light-drop hung by
cable to fill rooms

- light falling
upward yet anchored
to pupil-dark at the heart

thus do i light me
& watch me burn this
small measure of body to

choose what i do by its light
before my white sliver
adrift with dark

sputters behind
far headlands bearing
one head with it - one dark

head leant into the stroke
& on the shore that
statued face

vacating &
where the buddha
smile was buoyed this

slight curvature of space

Mario Petrucci

Too Tired to Push

Maternity pads and funeral arrangements
are never a perfect combination,
but they have entered our lives:
become another part of the situation.

Why are prams and pushchairs everywhere
whenever I walk about the streets?

Why do people say we should talk,
when we have not stopped, nor cannot sleep.

And as a way of making contact
people say they understand the way we feel.
Not a good thing to say. Because you don't
and I hope and pray you never will.

Jeremy Young

i have a bay

in me
whose walls
gaze out fresh as

milk to draw a tongue
of ocean lapping -
where eye

levels
horizon to
raise the bowed &

one spireless geometry
ushers this body
to its cooler

shadow
where dusk
touches my dusk

as absent-minded
& slack as a
lover

whose
desire is
single flame

by which i see -
one candle
set & lit

for me

Mario Petrucci

COWS

There are splits in reality
I saw them
It was really annoying
This is my alternative universe
And I don't trust it
So I dream of other worlds
What are they like?
Don't ask
But you weren't asking anyway

I saw somebody yesterday
I don't understand him
He might be an alien
But I don't think so
So I don't ask
What's it all about then?
I don't care
I gave up caring long ago

I used to pray sometimes nights
Till they proved God was insane
But I don't believe them
I think he's just really pissed off
He's probably dead normal really
What are you playing at then?
I asked him
But he couldn't talk
He gave up talking long ago

Never is a very long time
A very very long time
Meanwhile I'm reading Nietzsche
I've read eight pages
Lots of times
Seems he cracked up in the end
And asked
"Why am I so bloody ace?"
But no-one was interested

When I'm bored I talk
Loudly in my head
I used to talk to walls
So I never know if anyone hears me
But I don't bother asking
If they can
It's all part of growing up
The destruction of possibilities.

Andrew Mottram

at waters' meet

a heron stands
intent
its silhouette
against
the sheen
of evening
still

between
the rivers' meet
the fisher's feet
washed
by rain
from purpled
hills
on either hand

the land
goes
yawning
into
sleep

Milner Place

CATHERINE

As they left they pinned me to the door-frame,
set me grinning, sparking in amber-red and gold,
in case they called in, felt drawn to the hearth,
its glowing coals, its scattering of the cold.

They'll watch. I'll skywrite in loops of fire,
veer off, spin a still point, then corkscrewing down,
extinguish in November leaves by the door
of that strange and secret place called home.

Chris Bousfield

Just Off

Plaza Ana
Antonio Serrano is playing jazz harmonica.
Rough glamour in a wiry lick of hair
over one eye kind of way.
The grey beard at the piano
follows him everywhere,
over the mountains, wooded river banks,
sharp-scented orange groves of the travelling music,
into every dark bar,
through cool night streets
into the smoky bedrooms of the winding music.

There is a girl behind a pillar.
The cigarette she holds is longer than her fingers.
She is the only one not gazing at Antonio.
He leaves the stage to the trio,
fixes his mouth on the girl's.
Piano, bass, stark drum solos play themselves out
through the long long long exposition
of his kiss.

Mandy Oates

Laying Out

Ten miles past Cherbourg
the 2CV gutters to the side of the road.
In the small hours
we lay out the four squashed children
in a row on the verge,
book end them in the dark
and sleep deep as night.

At first light he walks away swinging the red can
till as a speck he disappears round the curve of the road.
The children still on the grass
curled like beans, their cool limbs white,
the fragile rise and fall of their breathing,
their long eyelashes trembling with dreams.
Sunflower fields to right and left.

All those yellow suns.

Mandy Oates

the black ewe

they always said
she'd come
to a bad end

they're dead

she sits
in a rocker
counting
her evils
knits a shawl
from days

grinning
she sniffs
the perfumes
in old lusts
passions
skin to skin
fierce grip
of thighs

drinks herself
from laughter
into dreams
sunsets
where crimson
of dead clouds
sits
over islands
drifting into haze

she rows a river
flowing sweet
rocks to music
scored
by the lord
of years.

Milner Place

till death

a cold clean wind
sliding
off the sierra
a far village
white as snow

her lips
wet with wine
her perfume
close music

no forgetting

Milner Place

KANDINSKY'S DEATH POEM

At Kandinsky's death bed he might have said something
essential to the development of human knowledge and
understanding.

But he probably didn't.

He probably said something about being a mere
triangle
in the dark void of time, destined to decay into an ever
decreasing circle and blink out of existence like a dot
flash of light on an offturned television set.

But I don't know because I wasn't there.

So I can only guess.

I'm not that interested in what went off in his head.

Though he probably was.

So he tried to tell us in his paintings.

"Circles and Triangles."

He said.

"Circles and Triangles collapsing and fading in
multicoloured disuniformity, within the deep black chaotic
nothingness of misunderstanding. This is the basic nature of
life. This is the answer."

But no-one was much interested in the question.

And he died just the same.

Andrew Mottram

The Verger's Goat

His hooves leave a clear sharp print.
They stamp down,
are individually fashioned.
    Over the years they wear.
    Their edges become less precise

His horns are lethal weapons
borne with pride; they will wound
enemy or friend; on show
    they are polished, ornamental,
    but don't ever trash them.

His left eye is pale, blind.
It changes its shape,
looks on lovers without curiosity;
    like a balloon it floats,
    like a sickle it is clean-edged.

It stares through a cloud,
Its movements can be predicted
but still they surprise us;
    in daylight it is transparent.
    He crops to the right.

His coat is yellowish.
Fragments of food are trapped in it
He stinks. He is unseemly, unkempt.
    His beard is an affront, not donnish
    It wields an obscene fascination.

Half-mad, he all the same knows his mind.
He hides in ditches.
He brings unwanted news.
    His selfhood is not to be shaken.
    He is accountable only to God

Gerard Benson